Shakespeare's Will

Shakespeare's Will

Vern Thiessen

Playwrights Canada Press
Toronto • Canada

PLAYWRIGHTS CANADA PRESS
215 Spadina Avenue, Suite 230, Toronto, Ontario, Canada M5T 2C7
phone 416.703.0013   fax 416.408.3402
info@playwrightscanada.com • www.playwrightscanada.com

For professional or amateur production rights, please contact:
Kensington Literary Representation
34 St. Andrew Street, Toronto, ON M5T 1K6
phone: 416-979-0187   email: kensingtonlit@rogers.com

Playwrights Canada Press acknowledges the financial support of the Government
of Canada through the Canada Book Fund and the Canada Council for the Arts
and of the Province of Ontario through the Ontario Arts Council and the
Ontario Media Development Corporation for our publishing activities.

Front cover image: *Woman by the Sea* by Sarah Brayer, aquatint, edition 22, 2001.
Production Editor: Michael Petrasek
Cover design: JLArt and Vern Thiessen

LIBRARY AND ARCHIVES CANADA CATALOGUING IN PUBLICATION
Thiessen, Vern
Shakespeare's will / Vern Thiessen. -- 2nd ed.

A play.
ISBN 978-0-88754-769-0

1. Hathaway, Anne, 1556?-1623--Drama. I Title.

PS8589.H4524S48 2007   C812'.54   C2007-906293-8

Second, revised edition: December 2007
Second printing: August 2011
Printed and bound in Canada by AGMV Marquis, Montreal

Table of Contents

No Book has yet been written
in praise of a woman who
let her husband & children
Starve or Suffer while she
Invented even the most useful
things, or wrote books,
or expressed herself in art,
or evolved philosophic systems.

—Anna Garlin Spencer

Love rests on no foundation.
It is an endless ocean,
with no beginning or end.
Imagine,
a suspended ocean,
riding on a cushion of ancient secrets.
All souls have drowned in it,
and now dwell there.
One drop of that ocean is hope,
and the rest is fear.

—Mowlana Jalaluddin Rumi

I believe that what woman resents is not so
much giving herself in pieces as giving herself
purposelessly.

—Anne Morrow Lindbergh

Acknowledgements

It takes many people and organizations to help a playwright create, develop, and produce a new play. The playwright thanks the Free Will Players/River City Shakespeare Festival for commissioning the play. Thanks also to the Alberta Foundation for the Arts, the Canada Council for the Arts, the Winspear Fund, the ATP/Banff playRites Colony 2004, Alberta Playwrights Network, the Lee Fund, Epic Theatre Ensemble, Metro Stage, Theatre 40, and the Citadel New Play Development program for assisting in the writing and development of this play.

Thanks must go to the following individuals for their inspiration, support, help and commitment to both myself and the project: Eden Philp, Ruth Dyckfehderau, Margaret Reed, Lisa O'Connell, Brian Dooley, John Kirkpatrick, John Murrell, David Brundage, James MacDonald, Maureen Labonté, Mark Haroun, Sharon Richardson, Holly Hoover, Vanessa Sabourin, Playwrights Canada Press, Seana McKenna, Miles Potter, Susan Bay Nimoy, Leonard Nimoy, JeanMarie Simpson, and Michael Petrasek.

Thanks also to Bob Baker for the risks he takes in nurturing and producing new plays, and to the Citadel Theatre audiences who have been so supportive of my work in recent years.

A special thanks must go to Geoff Brumlik for his dedication, and for his enthusiasm and passion for the play.

Shakespeare's Will was commissioned by Free Will Players, in 2002. It premiered in 2005 at the Citadel Theatre, Edmonton, Alberta, Canada, produced by the Citadel in association with Free Will Players. It was performed on the Rice Stage with the following company:

ANNE   Jan Alexandra Smith

Directed by Geoffrey Brumlik
Set & Costume Design by Guido Tondino
Lighting Design by Del Surjik
Sound Design/Composer: Dave Clarke
Asst. Set & Costume Design by Victoria Zimski
Stage Managed by Michelle Chan
Apprentice Stage Manager: Shannon Macelli
Choreography: Anita Miotti

——————————— • • • ———————————

This version of the play was developed for the Stratford Festival of Canada, and opened in June 2007 with the following company:

ANNE   Seana McKenna

Directed by Miles Potter
Designed by Peter Hartwell
Lighting Design by Kevin Fraser
Composer: Marc Desormeaux
Sound Design by Peter McBoyle
Stage Managed by Anne Murphy
Assistant Stage Manager: Kim Lott
Production Assistant: Lucy Martin
Production Stage Manager: Marylu Moyer

Shakespeare's Will had its American premiere at Theatre 40 in Los Angeles, California, in June 2007, with the following company:

ANNE   JeanMarie Simpson

Directed by Susan Bay Nimoy
Produced by Leonard Nimoy
Stage Management & Set Design by Crystal M. Munson
Lighting Design by Ellen Monocroussos
Sound Design by Marc Olevin
Costume Design by Shon Leblanc and Perry Ash
Make-up and hair by Debbie San Filippo and Carol Romano
Choreography by L. Martina Young
Production Assistant: Katrien Damman

Characters

ANNE: a woman of indeterminate age.

Setting

Anne's room, her imagination, her memory, her dreams, and the sea.

Style

Although the language is poetic in structure—and the play somewhat based on historical incidents—it should be played without sentimentality, reverence, softness or overt attempts at historical accuracy. Rather, theatricality, humour, brashness, and non-realism in acting, lighting, set, costume, movement and music/sound design is encouraged.

Dialects are not to be used.

The play runs approximately one hour and 30 minutes without intermission.

Movement, Music, Songs

These sections of the play are essential to the play's rhythm and must not be omitted. They "cleanse the pallet" and provide important emotional transitions for the audience, and the character of Anne. The "gist" of the music/movement is suggested in this text, but it may be as theatrical as is desired. Music inspiration for these sections include time-honoured songs such as "Miri It Is," "Scarborough Fair," "I Saw My Lady Weep" and "She Moves Through the Fair" to the more modern: "Kindertotenlieder" of Gustav Mahler and the songs of Ralph Vaughan Williams. In the text of this edition, all lyrics are those composed for the premiere production by Geoff Brumlik, and are used here with permission. Music is by Dave Clarke, who can be contacted at stancat@shaw.ca.

Note to Producers

Please consult with the playwright, his agent, or the publisher for the most recent version of the script. Should Geoff Brumlik's lyrics be used in production, he is to be credited in the house program.

SHAKESPEARE'S WILL

Rain.

She moves slowly through it.

She enters her house.

She stares at her room.

ANNE   I long for the sea....

Her white toothed smile.
Her roaring laugh.
Her salt spray on my lips....

(wry) The sea was a far better lover than you, Bill.
When it had me
I was wet and warm.

But you:
you
were a rough rocky shore
your head worn by tide
your beard straggly as seaweed
your eyes...

> *A distant bell. She listens.*
>
> *She puts down the will.*
>
> *She lights a lamp.*
>
> *She removes her mourning attire.*
>
> *She stares out the window.*

I buried you in the church
only this morning.
Fifty-two of the town's poorest
one for every year of your life
lead the way
hired to mourn your passing.
Then
two score men
riding the finest geldings
sinking in the soft mud.
Then

a dozen more
walking
the banner of arms
hanging heavy in their wet hands.
Then you
in a wagon covered with black velvet.
And then
I
and your friends from the city
and your family
trailing behind
grief
and the rain
weighing us down
soaked through we are
soggy as the sea.

Pause.

After
as the men go to eat
and talk
and drink down your memory,
your sister Joan
hands me your will:

She looks at the will.

Come Anne, says Joan
You must go home straightaway
Oh? I say
I'll be by tonight, she says.
Why, I say?

And she smiles
smiles
like....

A distant bell. She listens.

And now. An hour left
till Joan comes
only an hour
and I haven't even...

She regards the will.

* * * *

* *Movement/Music Sequence:*

Perhaps a lively, traditional song. Perhaps "The Fair."

(*sings*) "The boys, the boys, the boys of the town
They're pretty, and witty and brave.
They dance like the wind, and they kiss like the sea
And soon 'twill be my heart they crave, they crave
And soon 'twill be my heart they crave.
The boys, the boys, the boys of the town
Are back now from riding the waves
They'll love you so true, 'til the first morning dew
But then 'twill be elsewhere they'll crave, they'll crave
But then 'twill be elsewhere they'll crave."

The song swings her into the past.

A country town, like any other.
A square, with market.
A High Street, with shops.
(*smiles*) I meet you
at the yearly fair
in summer.
Shading our eyes
from the afternoon's sleepy sun.
We watch the players
in from the City
don't remember the name of it
don't care, really.

We stand side by side.
We watch a fat actor
play the part
of a fat actor
and you laugh
and I laugh too
more at you
than the play.

* See production notes on Movement/Music, page vi.

Your eyes dancing
your slender frame
hunched at the shoulders
your arms crossed
fingering your
thin red beard
dissecting every moment
your eyebrows knit
trying to understand
how it is stitched together
why it is
what it is.

(flirting) I'm Anne, I say.
(shy) Aye, you say.

> *Pause.*

Of Stratford, I say.
Aye, you say.

> *Pause.*

And you?
Bill.

> *Pause.*

Of…?
Same.

> *Pause.*

Do you come every year?
Aye.

> *Pause.*

To the Faire.
Aye.

> *Pause.*

To see the players.
Aye.

A man of few words, I think.
I like that.
I think.

* * * *

Later
in my father's barn
you fumble with my skirts.
Your hands, shaking
never having been
had
not by a woman at least
not by an older woman
at least.

Pause.

Afterwards:
you, staring at the stars
through the hole
in the barn roof
reliving the play
acting all the parts
making me laugh
more than I did at the fair.

Pause.

How old are you, I say.
Five and twenty, you say.
Liar, I say.
...Eighteen, you say.
(Oh Lord...)

And you?
...Older.
How much?
Older!
Thirty?
NO!
What then?
Six and twenty.
And I see

you look terrified
and very pleased with yourself
all in one.

You know, I say,
I don't want to marry.
Not you, not anyone.
I'm happy, I say,
to live with my father
and brothers
well-fed
well cared-for
much to do
with Mother gone
never wanted more.

Aye, you say,
me too.
Besides, you say,
I'm Catholic.
Catholic?
Aye.
Oh dear.
Aye.
I'm not.
Aye.

Besides, you say....
What...?
Nothing, I...
...What?
NOTHING!

> *Pause.*

Do you... I say
...do you...
What.
I don't know... like boys?
A long pause here.
...Don't know, you say.
Don't know?!
And I laugh

and laugh:
Don't know...?!

But then I see
you are hurt.
It's fine, I say,
doesn't matter,
doesn't matter
not to me.
Tell you a secret:
Me? I like boys too,
men that is
I like the company of lots and lots of men.
Why d'you think I go to the faire?

And your eyes smile
and you laugh
and I wipe away your tears
and we know
know
there is something...
something
between us.

* * * *

SHAKE-SPEARE!
My father is furious.
A *Shake-speare*!?
...Father....
The son of a glove maker?! The son of a papist who
can't pay his bills?!
The son of the WORST MAYOR WE EVER HAD?!
Father please!
What's he do then?
Tutor! I say, *(to impress)* in Lancashire.
LANCASHIRE! Dear poaching papists!
Father!
A *tutor*?! A *Catholic*!? And a *Shake-speare*!?
Jesus Christ! Jesus Christ in Heaven!

* * * *

But when two months pass
and no sign of blood
I know, I know
we are joined
forever
whether we like it
or not.

I'm with child, I say.

> *Pause*

Oh?

> *Pause*

Yes.

> *Pause*

What should we do, I say?
And you smile
smile
from ear to ear.
Get married?
Aye!!!
Aye!!
And we both
laugh and laugh....

* * * *

JESUS CHRIST!
Father.
WITH CHILD?!
Father.
You: six and twenty?! And him: barely eighteen?! And
both of you, with
NO MONEY?!
Father please.
You'll not be married in the Queen's church,
not on my life, not on my life, or your mother's certain to
RISE FROM THE DEAD TO SMITE US ALL!!
Father!
Marry a *Catholic*?! And *with child*?!

And to a *Shake-speare*?!
Jesus Christ! Jesus Christ in Heaven!

* * * *

And so
three days later
off to Temple Grafton
five miles from town
on my father's horse.

My father
holding me round the waist
praying for forgiveness he is
from God
or my mother
I'm not sure which.
Me: a head crowned with garlands
and
a handful of rosemary.

Father and I race to get there.
Bad luck, he says,
bad luck to marry after the clock strikes noon

We stop along the way
twice
so I can retch
the morning sickness
already upon me.

We arrive as
the church bell
tolls eleven.

But you...
you do not arrive 'til two.

My father
is fit to be tied.
Visions drift past his eyes:
You: drawn and disemboweled.
You: hanged and quartered.
You: beheaded and burned.
But a sideways glance from me

stays your execution
to a later date.

With you
your best friend:
Hamnet Saddler
the baker from town
on a horse
spotted with flour.
Chubby and clean
dressed in his finest
he is today
"official wedding witness."

And you.
You.
Your beard waxed
your clothes fresh
though your eyes are red
from too much ale, I presume.
Still, they sparkle
like Venus at dusk.

The priest
(John Rith by name)
deemed unsound by some,
"unsound" meaning Catholic.
His nose red with spirits
his breath reeks
so strong of Madeira
I think he himself has been bottled in Portugal.
And when the moment comes
you give me no ring.
I'll buy you one later, you say,
when we have money
I promise.
When we have money.

       Pause.

Father Rith blesses us
and when we exchange the vows
you kiss me.

And now
I see
the red
is not from drink at all
but from tears.

I love you,
you say,
I love you so.

* * * *

Alone that night
in your parents' house
you take out a sheaf of paper

She picks up a sheaf.

and read to me
some words
words:

* "Those lips that Love's own hand did make
Breath'd forth the sound that said I hate
To me that languish'd for her sake:
But when she saw my woeful state,
Straight in her heart did mercy come.
Chiding that tongue, that ever sweet
Was used in giving gentle doom:
And taught it thus anew to greet:
'I hate' she alter'd with an end
That follow'd it as gentle day
Doth follow night, who like a fiend
From heaven to hell is flown away.
'I hate' from hate away she threw,
And sav'd my life, saying 'not you.'"

Pause.

…Well…
Do you like it? you say.
It's… it's beautiful.
It's about you.
Oh?
"'I hate' from hate away she threw,

* *Sonnet 145*

And sav'd my life, saying 'not you'."
"Hate away," "Hatheway," you see?
(charmed) Oh...
One day, you say,
one day, I shall write better.

And then
you hold out your hand
and I mine
and sitting on the bed
We make a vow:

To live our own lives.
To treat each other well
but allow for our
separate desires.
To have our secrets
but protect
what we each
hold most dear.

It will be
our own kind of marriage.

           * * * *

       Music/Movement Sequence:

       She dances with an imaginary Bill, her movement
       echoing their passion. Perhaps a haunting melody,
       perhaps "Rushes."

(sings) "On a soft bed of rushes
With my lover I lay
When a sweet tide of passion
Did whirl us away...
Warm waters swirled round us
From north and from south
My breast on his bosom
My mouth on his mouth..."

       The bell invades. Rain.

I buried you in the church
only this morning

with that stupid headstone
with that stupid inscription
insisted on
by your stupid sister Joan.

> *She picks up the will.*

You must go home straight away, she says.
Oh? I say
I'll be by tonight.
Why I say?
Have you not read it? she says
No, I say.
And I shant.
And she smiles
smiles
like....

> *She considers it. Lets it rest.*

No.
No.
Not now....

* * * *

> *Her mind moves to the past. Perhaps she finds a
> child's dress.*

Seven months, Bill. Married seven months,
and still living with your father.

It is shortly after noon
I in the kitchen
and you out
busy with your pupils
(I think)
when
inside me
something bursts
and I fall
the water running down
and I know
know
Susanna

inside me
is saying
I am coming.
Now. I am coming.

Your mother gathers
women from the town
(except Joan, who
like you
is no where to be found).
She has gathered them to help
And when you do finally arrive
they bar your entrance
to the house
send the men to get you drunk.
And countless hours later
after all the pain and pushing and Please God Let It Come,
Susanna
awash in blood and phlegm and
and every inch of my insides
slides
out of me
like a seal
as if
born in the water herself.
Thus she comes to us
Bill.

A child cries.

I do not know how
to hold a child
rock it to sleep.
My mother taught me nothing of children.
She died before she could teach me
how to hold it
calm it
speak to it
when it wants not to lay down.

I shake my head:
no don't cry

no
a nap, you need to nap,
to sleep is good! it's good!
Suddenly knowing
why mothers of old
threw their children from windows
left them to die on mountaintops
buried them under pillows.
Quiet, I say.
Quiet.
But to no avail.

Enough, I say.
Enough!
To no avail.

BAD GIRL, I say.
BAD!
To no avail.

She wants my breast
but will not suck
and when finally she does,
my nipple
raw like a skinned knee
chokes her
drowns her in my milk,
and she cries more.

And then I hear it
the sound of...
No... No...
But there it is:
Shite.
Yellow, brown, runny SHITE
everywhere
on my arms
on my lap
on my fingers
and I
I am
COVERED IN SHITE.

And now she is SCREAMING
and crying
and
and
And now I cry
cry like a child myself
cry....

And I, I,

I must do something
focus the mind
sink the screams
loud as any gull.
And so I rock her
I rock her
and say:
(gently) Shhh....
Shhh....

And like the sea sweeping the shore...

Shhh

...soft as surf on sand...

Shhh...

...she drifts off....

The sweet silence of sleep.

Saved I am.

Saved by the sea.

       Pause.

And when
almost three years later
in our own tiny house in town
Judith and Harry come to us
they come together
and I
I am glad simply to be alive.
The women of the town
wide-eyed and whispering

amazed I have survived
the birth of twins.
A miracle! they say,
a girl AND a boy! Praise God!

And you....
You are so happy.
To have a son

a son
(as well as another girl, of course, of course)
but a son!
A son!

                    * * * *

At night
when all the children are asleep
I watch
as you start writing
late at night
poem after poem
reading them to anyone who will listen:
me
your pupils
Gnasher, the dog.

And then
for the first time
with homemade poppets
you make up plays
act them out
to make Susanna laugh.
Susanna: Your little poppet.

          Pause.

The summers come
and with them the Faire
and with the Faire
the players.

You begin missing work
your pupils wondering where you are
and I saying you are ill

while you run to the square to
see all the plays
three days straight
never coming home nights
drinking with the actors
at the Bull's Head:
devising plots
making rhymes
building characters
in your mind.

And I keep my promise
to allow you your life.
Even when
the children wonder
where you are
even when
I am exhausted from worry
even when
at night
the children asleep
I sit
alone
by the fire
try to remember
what it was like
to be
not a mother
but a woman
wanting nothing more
than for you
to hold me
talk with me.
Even then
I keep my vow.

Pause.

Then
one night
(Susanna three, the twins barely a year)
you stumble home

drunk
not with ale
but with a future.

A position, you say
I've been offered a position!
With the Queen's Men
at first as a player
but later, perhaps later
as a writer,
a writer!!

The excitement in your voice
the joy in your eyes
the thrill in your hands
as they dance their ideas in the air.

I'll come back every month, you say.
I'll make ten shillings a week
ten shillings!
That's more than I make now!
I'll send home money!

Please, you say,
please....

>   *She sighs.*

I am doubtful.

Trust me, you say.
Trust you?
Aye, you say, trust me.
You in the City and me here
with three children?
Your father'll help, you say.
Oh my father *loves* you.
Stop it.
Going off to be a writer, oh he'll love that.
Stop it!
Trust you?
STOP IT!

>   *Pause.*

How can I?
How can I trust something
I don't understand?
How can I....

Pause.

And then. You speak, you say:
(gently) Listen to me.
Anne.
Listen.
We are different than others.
Since we first met
you've guided our way
done what's right:
marriage
children
work
and you being older
wiser
I trusted you.
I trusted you, Anne.
And now
now
you must trust me
But how, I say
how do I do that?
From here, you say
from the heart.

She sighs again.

Six months, I say.
THANK YOU!
Six months!
and then we shall see!

Thank you, thank you! And you
kiss me
hug me
and I can see the tears
well up like waves
behind your eyes.

You shan't regret this, you say
you shan't.
Don't worry
don't
I will be back anon.

Does that mean soon? I say.
It means...
what it means.

* * * *

Jesus Christ!
Father.
A PLAYER?!
Father.
A CATHOLIC, a TUTOR, a SHAKE-SPEARE, and now
AN AC-TOR!?
Father please.
JESUS CHRIST! JESUS CHRIST IN HEAVEN!

* * * *

Two days later
you borrow a horse
from Hamnet Saddler
your bag stuffed
with half-written plays and poems
Susanna on my hip
the twins with my father.

We kiss
Once.
Twice.
I leave, then
run back to
kiss you again.

You look at me
your eyes wet as the day.

Don't forget me, I say,
don't forget me.

You try to speak
but...
all you can do...
...is wave.

* * * *

Music/Movement Sequence:

*She waves goodbye, Susanna on her hip. Perhaps
a melancholy song. Perhaps "My Love Doth Fly."*

(*sings*) "My love doth fly on golden wing
With golden note my love doth sing
My love doth light on highest bower
And chimes my name out every hour.
My love doth soar through golden skies
On golden breeze my love doth glide
My love doth skim o'er golden sea
and thus, so golden, my love comes to me."

> *As the sequence progresses, the wave of her hand
> transforms into a flood of memory....*

* * * *

Six months pass
and I agree to another six months.
Then another
And another
'til the years blend
like sand on a shore.
Our separate lives....

> *Perhaps she spots some toys. Perhaps a doll:*

Susanna shoots up
taller and taller
but is still your little poppet
lanky and thin
like the willow in front of our house
her hair
falling past her eyes
her long arms

bending like a branch
to pick up Catter, meowing.

Joan says
she is always sad
but I say no
she is only quiet
like her father
holding secrets in her eyes.

> *Next, a carving, perhaps of a hen.*

And then Judith
like the firecrackers
we see from China
twirling
popping
she explodes here and there.
She has taken
to talking to the chickens
chasing the hens round the yard
naming them
speaking to them
teaching them
how to best lay eggs
demonstrating
by SITTING ON THEIR EGGS FOR THEM,
after which
she gets into a fight with me
her bottom yellow
dripping with yolk.
And so it is I call her my chick.
Judith, my chick, chick, chick.

> *Next, a child's model ship.*

And of course, Hamnet.
The flip side of his twin.
He tumbled out last
but insists
on being first in everything else.
Hamnet is a stupid name
don't you think?

Very
I don't know,
German
or something.
"Hamnet" after your best friend Saddler.
Might as well call him Cornelius or Oswald
or something.
He hates it too
asks can I change it?
I like Harry, Mother, call me that
and so I do.

Judith came into the world crying
but Harry?
Silent as a lamb.
Well built and strong,
strong in spirit, strong in mind.
He is a rock
standing tall against any wave
shining when life's sea
splashes against him
glistening in the sun
even when...
even when....

> *Pause.*

Harry likes to build things.
Not plays like you
but ships.

He dreams of the sea
of visiting far off lands
whittling boats
from any piece of wood he can find.
Collecting rocks from the yard
to fashion a harbour
old cloth from my washing
to cut into sails
stick sailors from splinters of firewood
cork from Sunday's sherry
to float them

'til he has built enough
Victorys, Triumphs, and *Golden Lion*s
to battle any Armada.

He plays with Saddler's son
carefully carrying their prize creations
down to the river.
They run along the banks
to watch their ships' journey.

And should a ship run aground
or disappear
in an eddy
or whirlpool
or the reeds
Harry never curses,
Bill. Never.

No, he simply runs back home
builds another ship
to save the old one
from sinking
to a watery tomb.

> *Pause.*

Your prize ship, Bill.
Your prize.

> *The bell and the rain return her to the present.*

* * * *

Your sister Joan
is a bitch.

I'm sorry but she is.
She is bitter and nosey
and at the funeral
talks of nothing but you
never once asking about me
never once asking about the children
never once....

> *She picks up the will. Puts it down.*

Have you not read it? she says.
No, I say,
and I shan't.
It's all written down, she says,
It's all there in steadfast ink.
And she smiles
smiles
like....

Pff.
What does she know, eh?
Of us.
Our lives....

           She laughs.

                    * * * *

And when you buy me a new house
this house Bill
Joan is FURIOUS.

He must be doing well,
she says.
Yes, I say.
Very well, she says
her eyes green
as we watch men from town
deliver....
Built chairs?!
To replace old stools.
Stitched rugs?!
To replace loose rushes.
Oak shutters?!
To replace flimsy pine.

And our bed
now stuffed with soft feathers
instead of scratchy straw,
the children
so excited to
have beds of their own.

And I hire two servants,
Brundage and Nelly.

Nelly helps
to tend
the ox and hens
the goats and swine
the peacocks and pigeons
her arms sinewy and strong
as any mare.

Brundage pulls white water lilies
from our pond
and helps tend the garden:
Snapdragons and
Columbines
Daisies and
Marigolds
Sneezewort and
Yarrow
his fingers thin and delicate as
any stem.

Brundage wants to marry Nelly
desperately
but he is too shy to ask
and she too shy to say a word.
They live together
here as husband and wife
and yet I have never heard them say the words
I love you.
Never slept in the same bed
…I don't think.

Perhaps Bill
Perhaps
Like us
They have made their own vows.

Two servants!?
Joan cannot contain
the bile brimming on her lips:
To do WHAT? she says.

To WORK, I say.
Oh! says Joan.
Oh!
And she scuttles off
like a spider running from rain.

   Pause.

We become a kind of family:
The children and I and Brundage and Nelly.

The children are proud of their horses
Brundage of his ale,
Nelly of her butter
and I
I
I am proud of the excellence in our honeybees.

Bees love gossip, as you know Bill.
It is considered lucky to tell the bees
every bit of news.
If you don't
they may leave
and take their good luck with them.
So I must tell them all my secrets.
And so I do:

    * * * *

I say to them, I say:

My friends, my friends....
(the joy of telling a secret) I like men.
Many men.

It is a funny thing, my friends
I have only now discovered
being married
it is far more respectable to have many lovers.
When you are young and active
you are called
a slut
or a whore
or a strumpet
but once you are married

you are seen merely as
"dissatisfied"
or "unfaithful" or
"adventurous."
Silly
how we want to rob a young woman of her desire
and make her unwhole.

And now
with this new house
and servants
and time
I am again able to entertain the company of men.
Many men.
Men like Richard… Frederick… Alexander….

Alexander is young.
A fruit seller at the market
he likes to touch
and taste
and tease me.
But.
He thinks he knows what he wants
more than he does
and in truth needs another season
to fully ripen.

Now Matthew…
Matthew helps with the horses
and like his steeds
has much to be thankful for
between his legs.
Alack, he has
nothing so large between his ears.

And then there is Caleb.
Caleb is a stranger
passing through town
he knocks on my door
looking for a night's lodging
in the barn.

Rough face
rough mind
chest like a shelf
stomach like a rock
and his hands
hmm.
He speaks little
but his fingers
his mouth
his tongue
say more than any words.
I am wet well before the rain beats down on the barn roof,
the sharp smell of straw caught in my throat.

Come 'ere, he says
and I obey
come 'ere, he says
and I act defiant
pretending to struggle
wanting to be had.
But then
I turn the tables
ride him like my horse
control him
the reign of my hand
grabbing his long mane
galloping
through his flesh 'til he is snorting
and thirsty and sweating with exhaustion
begging for rest.

And then I slap his rear
and he canters off
never to return.

It's a funny thing,
my friends,
how once you've had them
they either lose interest completely
or want to marry you.
Never in between.

Always racing to the future,
never enjoying the present.

> *Pause.*

And yet
my friends
for all this…
for all this….

I miss my husband.
Not a man
but a husband.

A husband who is…
present.
Not "Here."
But "Present."
A difference.

What is it about men?
Eh? What is it?

But the bees never answer.
Only hum
in their hive.

* * * *

The more you succeed, Bill
the less and less you come home.

At first it was every month,
then every three
then on holy days to see the children,
then once when a bout
of the Fever
briefly closes the theatres,
once when your father died,
once for your mother,
sadly Joan lives on in perpetuity.

I become a beggar for news
asking anyone who comes from the City:
Do you have any word from my husband?
Yes, his play is doing well, they say.

Yes, I know, but my husband, do you have word from him?
You should be proud, they say.
Yes, I am, but has he sent word.
But now you write even less than you visit
saving your words only for work.
Only shillings arrive,
shillings and short messages:

She pulls some from the table.

"Dearest Anne:
All well here.
Will write later with details
Much Love
Bill."

Or:

"Dear Anne:

Send Hamnet and the girls my best.
Love
Bill."

Or:

"Anne:
Home next month.
Bill."

But you never come.

* * * *

At night...

I dream...

I am a gull
flying over
rocks, land
sliding down creeks, rivers, and roads
soaring into the City
to land atop the theatre.

I perch myself above the crowds
to see your newest

to see the players
to hear your words.

I watch them float up
the words
your words
and I
I snatch them in my beak
warm them under my wing.
take them back to my nest
and like juicy worms
feed them to the children
who gobble them down.
The words.
Your words.

                    * * * *

And when
finally
you DO come
it's unannounced
a surprise.

For "Hamnet's birthday,"
you say.
And Judith's, I say.
Of course
and Judith's....

            Pause.

And to see you playing with Harry.
Later
when the children are asleep
and we are alone
I say, I say:
Bill.
Bill.
It's time.

For what, you say.
It's time we came to live with you.
In the City.

Oh? you say.
Yes. We are coming to the City, Bill.
No, you say.
It's no place to raise children, Anne.

There are plenty of children in the City, Bill.

Is that what you want? you say,
Is that what you really want?
Do you really want the children to see
women whoring on the streets?
Do you want them to smell Fleet Ditch
stinking to high heaven?
Do you want them to watch men
begging in the streets?
To see sometime criminals
chained to the banks of the river?
To watch them die by the washing of three tides?
Do you really want the children to see these things, Anne?
Do you?

But that's not it.
You have secrets.
I know it.
I have heard talk
of a friend
a companion
in the City.
A man.
And that's fine
for I have secrets of my own
and best we leave them
for the bees.

I miss you, Bill.
Aye…
I've had enough of this.
I want the children to know their father.
Aye…
Then let us come!

Anne…
you say.

Yes?
Our vow
to allow each other to live our own lives.
Yes?
To protect what we each hold most dear.
Yes?
I take care of you, Anne.
Yes, you take care of me and the children and I
I give you decency, respect, lineage—
No, Anne, you say.
No.
You give me more than that:
You give me my work.
You give me my life, Anne.
But my life.
In the City.

>   *Pause. She sighs.*

And so you go.
And so I stay.
And try
to trust what I don't understand
to respect
what I can't control
and to let go
what I want to save.

>   * * * *

>   *Movement/Music Sequence:*

>   *Her daily routine, methodical and efficient.*
>   *Perhaps an eerie, menacing song. Perhaps: "It*
>   *Scirtches and Scratches."*

(*sings*) "It scirtches and scratches
And claws at the door.
It nibbles through bedding and sheets.
It steals like a thief
Through the dead dark of night
And will gnaw on your bones while you sleep,
While you sleep
It will gnaw at your bones while you sleep..."

She flings open the windows of the past.

* * * *

A hot spring day
shedding its winter coat.
The town comes alive
with birds
the scent of lilac
a warm breeze.

> *Pause.*

I walk to the market
to buy cures:
Sage and Bay
for Susanna's headaches.
Saffron and Basil
for Father's heart.
Wormwood and mint
for Judith's ever sensitive stomach.

> *Pause.*

Walking home through the square
I pass by the church.

(suspicious) Outside
women praying
for sudden salvation,
men
mad with fear
lashing themselves
atoning for the evils of the world.

> *Pause.*

…this is not good…

> *Pause.*

Almost home, down the lane,
a scream.
A woman crying.
I see a man stumble from the door
coughing blood.

Don't touch me! he says.
Robert! she cries.
Don't touch me!
Go back woman! Go back!
Robert!
And people near
pull her away as
he stumbles toward the next lane
pistol in hand.
No! she cries, No!
Then a shot
and he is dead.

The next day
I open my door
and stare down the street
nearly empty
save the mayor's cart
pulling through town.
They stop by the house of the woman
and paint a cross of red on her door.

News sweeps the town like a tide.
I can smell it in the wind
the spring is hot and damp
Gnasher is barking at things not there
Catter is scratching the walls of the house.
It is just like…
It is just like….

* * * *

I am eight and my mother is ill.
You were lucky, Bill.
Born in the spring that year you were.
You were spared
then
when the Fever
fetched a third of the town.
A whole third.
But my mother….

Her skin
is like stew:
burn marks
the size of lentils
boiling
on her arms
she shivering
even with the sun so hot that summer.
Then
hazelnuts on her neck,
then
goose eggs on her back,
then blood
when she sneezes
then more
when she coughs
and then
then
Father knows
it is time.

Come now my sweetlings, he says,
come now.
And he settles us in
by the fire
and tells us stories
of the sea.

Father was a ship's boy
carefully tending the hourglass
turning it
and soon as the sand had run through
He would strike a bell
for all aboard to hear.
When not at the glass
Father made "the sand" for it:
taking old eggshells
scraping them
rubbing them
'til their sticky crust was gone
grinding them down

so thin
that they passed like sand
through a sieve.

And so
huddled by the fire
he tells us tales:
Of ports and pirates
of black armadas
attacking by morn
of angels
lighting the ship by night
of Grimsby and Liverpool
Scarborough and Hull
of Italy and Spain
India and Africa.
And we laugh and squeal
and cry and feel
we are safe
safe as sailing, he says,
safe as sailing when the wind is up.
No matter what happens sweetlings, he says,
when the wind is up
you move on.
You always move on.

And so to save ourselves,
he says,
we must leave
leave
your mother.

> *Pause.*

We travel to the sea
where Father spent his youth.
He builds a small cabin
where we are safe
away from the rats
breeding in the walls of our house.
We live there for three months
playing tag with the surf

building castles in the sand
the waves rocking us to sleep
like she was our mother.

But when cool autumn comes
we return from the sea
and watch
as Father
lights fire to our house
our mother
now dead
inside
the church bells tolling
tolling.

* * * *

And so
I examine the children
incessantly:
Lips
tongue
Fever
Nothing.
No cough
no sneezing
no diarrhea
nothing.

But then
I see it:
Gnasher.
Limping.
I take a cloth
carefully lift his paw.

A sore.
Could be nothing.
But...
But....

Pause.

Just then
Harry comes inside
holding a rat
Catter's snagged.
He's taken your old pocketknife
cut the rat through, examining its parts
his hands covered in blood.

WHAT ARE YOU DOING?
I say.
I grab the knife
careful to pick it up with a cloth
throw it out the door
I pull him to the basin
wash his hands with lye
to let him know I am serious.

NEVER! I say.
Mother! he says.
NEVER. TOUCH. THOSE. THINGS. NEVER.
Mother!
Do you want to turn out like grandmother?
…no…
Do you want that? Do you?
No.
Do you?
NO!

> *Pause.*

No.
Now is the time.
I will not live another Fever
I will not.

> *Pause.*

I find Brundage.
The carriage, I say.
Wot? he says
THE CARRIAGE!
Now? he says.
Go!
They're shutting the town tomorrow, ma'am.

Then we must leave tonight.
But, but where to, ma'am?
The sea.
The sea?! But that's, that's three days journey, ma'am!
Will you come?

A pause here.

Will you?
Ma'am I…
We need you.
I…
Please.

Pause.

And so he fetches the carriage.
And so we pack.

She does.

Coats and blankets.
Food and money.
Quill and ink.
Paper and seals.
Books and toys.

Mother?
Yes my Chick?
Where we going?
Away, Judith.
Where?
A trip, my Chick. Holiday.
To see Father?
Maybe…

Mother?
Yes, Harry.
Is Father dead?
Now why would you say such a thing?
All the children said
last week
before we had to stay inside
they said everyone in the big City is dead.
Well he's not.

How'd you know?
I know.
But how?

I know.

> *Pause.*

But I don't.
Bill.
Know.

> *Pause.*

Then Nelly.
A letter
from Master Will.
I snatch it from her fingers.
Finally.

Short as always:

"Dearest Anne:
Don't worry.
I am well.
Do what you must.
Much Love
Bill."

Thank God you're alive. Thank God. At least I know
that.

> *Pause.*

Last minute instruction to Nelly
out of the children's earshot:

> *She writes quickly on paper.*

Send this to my Father.
Yes ma'am.
Have him kill Gnasher.
But ma'am.
I know it's hard
but it must be done.
Yes ma'am.

Send this to Master Will
letting him know the children are safe.

Yes ma'am.
We'll be back. I promise.
But she swallows hard
fear in her eyes.

I kiss her cheek.
If she has it
I will die.
We all will.
But how can I not.
Kiss her.

Pause.

After midnight.
Brundage snaps the reigns
and the carriage is off.

We ride through the night
the decaying bodies
lie by the road
shadows in the moonlight.

What are those, Mother?
Nothing, Harry.
Are they dead?
No, they are sleeping,
and so should you.
Why are they sleeping outside? he says.
It's been hot, I say,
and it's cooler
to sleep out of doors.

At the edge of town
we are met by the mayor's guard.
I pay him off with jewellery.

Travelling through the night
through the countryside.
Each town
burning their dead

the fires
lighting our way.

                      * * * *

The second day:
the sun peaks from behind
the clouds.

Are we there yet?
they ask.
And I laugh
and say,
Soon, my sweetlings.
Soon we will be safe.
Safe as sailing when the wind is up.

               Pause.

And then
on the third day
the carriage stops.
I awake
and yawn and stretch
the children beside me.
And step down and I look to the horizon and I...
I....

               She sees it.

You never forget, do you:
when you first see it.

Its wide smile
its salty breath
its loud laugh
its broad brow,
broad
as the shoulders of my father.

I have not been to the sea
since my mother's death,
since I myself was a child
and now
here I am

back
with my own children.

And we stand
all of us
staring at the sea.

* * * *

Brundage sets up house
in our carriage
puts up a makeshift tent.
And we?
We run to the shore.

Susanna hunts for starfish
to send to you
little Judith in frilly hat
Harry launching his ships into oncoming waves
and I...
I...

I see her white-toothed smile
hear her roaring laugh
from deep in her belly
taste the shower of her spray
on my lips
feel her hands
scrubbing my skin clean.
And I say, I say:
(laughs) I know you!
I know you!

Mother?
Yes, Judith my chick?
What does Father look like?
Stupid! says Susanna, like his portrait!
Now now!
He looks like me! says Harry
Yes, he looks like you
but older.
But what does he LOOK like, really.
Well my sweetlings...
well....

She creates the portrait with found items:

Here we are at the sea yes?
Yes!
Then we will create our own portrait.
They laugh
yes, yes, let's.

His face is as shiny as the moss there on the hill.
And they all grab moss to create an outline of your face.

His eyes are like two shiny stones on the beach.
Harry carefully chooses two
and Susanna places them down.

His hair
—what's left of it—
(they laugh again)
is like the straggly seaweed there.
Judith scoops some of the slimy stuff and
we fashion a wig for you.

His beard is soft, like the rushes in the bush back there.
They all run to yank them up
and place them carefully on your chin.

Does he smile, Mother?
Yes, my chick, always.
And what's that like?
Like the sun dancing on water.
We can't collect that! they scream.
No, I say.
No you can't.
So you will have to imagine that, my sweetlings.

And when the portrait is done
we all sit on our haunches
and admire our art...

...'til the surf washes
your smile
out to the sea.

> *The bell. She looks around her room, the light now fading.*

* * * *

Your sister Joan
is a bitch
and chronically late
I might add.
Thank God,
thank God for that today
for I haven't even....

> *She fingers the will. Pause.*

Fifteen years since... I last went to the sea.
And then
last month
a note
announcing your return.
Your friends
from the city
throwing you a party
here
"in honour of your departure from the theatre."
You are coming back.
You.
Are coming back.

> *She begins to dress, for both Joan and his arrival.*

And so
I prepare a feast.
Joan insists on helping
but does nothing
only talks of you
and your successes
and your wealth
and your honours
and all your friends coming back with you
as if *I* didn't feel proud of you.

Joan fusses over every part of the feast
'til Brundage and Nelly
are set to commit murder.
How the sauces are too spicy
and the table settings too gauche

and *again*
telling me how badly I have raised the children
after all
Judith is now poor and plump
Susanna is married to an idiot
and Harry, Harry…
Well!

Joan has not worked a day in her life
never had a child
nor screwed a man.
Such living is unhealthy, Bill, truly, it is.

* * * *

And then
after a lifetime away
you finally come home.
Home.

Funny.
Nervous as a schoolgirl
I am.
Not sure why.

You arrive
in a horse-drawn carriage.
You climb the steps to the new house:
balding
older
your eyes squinting from decades
of writing by candlelight
your brow furrowed from
building and rebuilding
burnt theatres.

> *Pause.*

Hello Bill, I say.
Hello Anne.

> *Pause.*

Welcome home, I say.
Thanks.

Pause.

You look well, I say.
Thanks.

Pause.

As do you, you say.
Thanks.

Pause.

And we kiss.
The first time in many a year
and for a brief moment
it is as if
we are back at the faire.

Pause.

That night, we throw the party
the great feast for your
retirement.

Your friends arrive:
Saddler and Fletcher
and Julyus Shawe and John Robinson
and Robert Whattcott and John Hemings
and Richard Burbage and Henry Condell
and Francis bloody Bacon
(Lord but he is a tedious man!)
and you all drink and eat and talk of old times.
So many people
so much laughter
in a house
that has been quiet
for so long....

But you
you do not laugh much.
You are
sad
awkward
out of place

looking for a new audience
for your old stories.

Susanna and Judith
arrive
greet you graciously
but look at you strange
call you Bill.
More like an uncle now
than a father.
You ask them little
only
how are you faring
and
I trust all is well
fearing deeper questions
would bring answers
you would not know how to respond to.

Searching too, you are.
For him.
The one I was told of
but never met.
The one who died
last summer
in the City.

> *Pause.*

The next day
we travel to the graveyard
place garlands on our parents' graves.
Then
we go to the place
by the stream
underneath the ash.
But you stop.

No....
Bill.
No, you say,
I cannot.

Please, I say.
Please.
"For those things we hold most dear."

But you do not come
simply stand away
as I lay herbs from the garden:
Rosemary for remembrance
Sage for strength
Thyme for courage.
And Parsley
to take away bitterness.

               * * * *

A week ago
I help you to bed.
Sweat
drips down your balding head
past your cheek
like rain on the window.

I lay down beside you.
You are hot
as an oven
burning
even as
the night grows cold.
I close my eyes and....

            Pause.

And when I open them again
I know
I know
the night has swept you away.

I go to the window

            She does.

Rain.
And fresh cool air
washes into the room
and rushes out again

taking you with it.
And you are gone.

> *Pause.*

> *The bell. The rain.*

And now:
the tributes
the plans for a book and
the remounting of your plays.

I must play the widow.
It is so much like work
so boring
so precious
so...
not you.

Come, Anne, she says.
You must go home straight away.
Oh?
I'll be by tonight, she says.
Why?
Have you not read it? she says.
No, I say,
and I shan't.
It's all written down, she says.
It's all there in steadfast ink.
He never forgot you know, she says,
he never forgot.
And she smiles
smiles
like....

> *She picks up the will.*

But why.
Why would I read it?

No one knows Bill.
No one knows the vow we kept,
what we held most dear.
No one knows that
what mattered

between us
was not written on paper
but on our hearts.
Only I know
the words written there.

But read it now I must.

She reads.

"In the name of God, Amen.
I, William Shakespeare
of Stratford-upon-Avon
in the county of Warwick
gentlemen
in perfect health and memory..."

Yes yes yes....

"Item:
I give and bequeath unto my daughter Judith
one hundred and fifty pounds of lawful English
money...
...in discharge of her marriage portion..."

Ahh. Bribing her to marry, I see.

She flips forward a page.

"Item:
I give, will, bequeath, and devise
unto my eldest daughter Susanna...
to have and to hold
all during the term of her natural life,
all my goods, chattel, leases, plate, jewels, and household stuff whatsoever.
And after her decease
to the first son of her body lawfully issuing, and to the
heirs...

...male...

...of her body...."

Pause.

I see. Lineage.

She finds another spot.

"Item:
To Hamnet Sadler 26 shillings and eight pence to buy
him a ring....
And to my fellows in the theatre
John Hemings, Richard Burbage, and Henry Condell
26 shillings and 8 pence apiece
to buy them all rings...."

She rubs her ring finger.

Rings... *(wry)* even though... even though...!

She reads more.

"Item:
I give and bequeath
unto my said sister Joan
20 pounds
and all my wearing apparel
and I do will and devise unto her...

the house in Stratford...

wherein she may dwelleth
for her natural life...."

She re-reads this to herself, confused.

The house...
The house...?
But....

Pause.

"Item: I give unto my wife...."

She turns over the leaf, reads to self, then:

"I give unto my wife...
... my second best bed..."

Pause.

"...with the furniture...."

She flips the pages, but there is no more. Pause.

And so this is...
this is my, my....

"He never forgot you know.
He never...."

* * * *

(*steady*) It happened so silently
me reading
Susanna making sandcastles
Judith and Harry
playing together in shallow surf.

Judith runs in
teeth clacking like a skeleton
and I pull a blanket round her.
I look up
Harry is now twenty feet out
waving
laughing.

He mouths something
but the gull's cry
drowns him out

I wave back
shoo away a wasp
and look up again
to see him gone.

And I,
I think
but where, where,
and I look up and down the shore
but still he is, he is, and I just saw him, where?
and I run to the water's edge, call to him, and the girls
they splash in, and I say no, there are currents and I, I
look for Brundage to help but he, high above, on the cliff,
and I call for help, but he cannot hear me, and I turn back,
and I—

  She gulps air and plunges forward.

—rush into the sea, my gowns heavy with water, and
Susanna yells:
No!
You will sink mother
you will sink
and so I tear it off:
my gown, my shirt, my shoes, my...

> *She tears away some of her clothing.*

trying to
to become a fish
to swim to you.
Harry!!
Harry!!

> *She catches her breath.*

And he
waving goodbye
like you
at the road's end
pack slung over your shoulder
waving
waving....

> *Pause.*

For hours
I hoped
the ocean would take pity
throw him up
spout him out
like Jonah
alive.

> *Pause.*

And
to have Brundage
deliver him to me
pulled from a grave so wet.
And to hold him in my arms
to pull away the cold kelp
wrapped round his neck like a noose.

Pause.

And
not to bring him home
but instead to burn him on the beach that night
for his body, bloated had....

And
to carry his ashes
in a box cut from birch
to hold him on my lap one last time
three days back in the carriage
and to lower it in the ground
and to hear the church bell toll
like a ship
so far away, so far....

She grabs the will, her anger mounting.

And with this
you blame me?
with this you punish me?
with these words
you break it
our promise
with this
you rip in two
our vow
with this
you
you....

In a rage, she grabs the sheaves, but does not rip them.

No, no, no, no, no! I will not suffer this, I will not!

She tosses the will aside.

A long pause.

Then:

The bell.

But it seems far away. She listens.

I will go back.

      Pause.

Yes.

      Pause.

I will go back.

I will go back to the sea
to live like my father.
I will go back to the sea
to live where I last saw my son.
I will go back to the sea
to let the waves
wash my wounds clean
of consequence
of memory
of words.

      Pause.

"Those lips that Love's own hand did make
Breath'd forth the sound that said I hate...
'I hate' from hate away she threw,
And sav'd my life, saying 'not you'..."

      Pause.

To hell.
To hell with your words.

Sink them in the sea
drown them in the depths
smash them on the shore
let the waves carry them where they will.

(*smiles faintly*) For when the wind is up, you move on.

You always move on.

      The bell is clearer now.

      It is a ship's bell

      Its sound draws ever closer.

      End of Play.

Postscript

Shakespeare's Will is loosely based on the life of Anne Hathaway, the woman who married William Shakespeare. Or rather, the play is based on the very few facts we actually know about Anne. Controversy surrounds many aspects of Anne's life, but historians tend to agree on the following:

- Anne married Shakespeare when she was twenty-six years old. He was eighteen.

- She was pregnant at the time of the wedding.

- They had three children: Susanna, and twins Hamnet & Judith.

- Anne lived her life in Stratford-Upon-Avon.

- Shakespeare spent most of his adult life in London.

- Hamnet died at age 11. It is not known how he perished, although there is a record of the plague sweeping the town at that time.

- Shakespeare returned to Stratford some time after 1610.

- Shakespeare died in Stratford in 1616 at age 52.

- Anne died in Stratford in 1623 at age 67.

- Joan died in 1646 at age 77.

- Susanna died in 1649 at age 66 leaving no male heir.

- Judith died in 1662 at age 76 leaving no male heir.

- Shakespeare indeed had a will.

The sections Anne reads at the end of the play are quotes from the will. These passages of the will became my primary inspiration in writing the play.

Scholars have long debated Shakespeare's directive "I give unto my wife my second best bed with the furniture." Samuel S. Schoenbaum, author of *William Shakespeare: A Documentary Life*, suggests that it would have been Anne's right, through English common law, to one-third of his estate. He also suggests that the best bed was reserved for guests, and thus the "second best bed" was a meaningful gift of their marriage bed. Joyce Rogers in *The*

Second Best Bed: Shakespeare's Will in a New Light also concludes that the will was correct, incontestable, conventional, and designed to serve the best interests of the women and children in his family. Others maintain the will was a slight on Anne. The 18th century scholar, Edmund Malone, appears indignant that Shakespeare cut off Anne, "not indeed with a shilling, but with an old bed." More recently, the actor Sir Ian McKellen has argued that the playwright's decision of what to leave Anne showed he had a lack of interest in her and the marriage. And still, others believe, as Willard McCarty of King's College London, that all the debate surrounding Shakespeare's private life doesn't really matter to the study of Shakespearean literature, and therefore the question of the will's meaning is moot.

What we know about the creation of the will is also scant. By most accounts, William Shakespeare began finalizing his last will and testament in early 1616. It appears Francis Collins of Warwick acted as Shakespeare's attorney. Shakespeare made corrections and additions to the will and five witnesses signed the official version in March 1616. The original copy of Shakespeare's will is three large sheets of paper bound together by a narrow strip of parchment at the top margins with each page signed by Shakespeare himself.

A version of Shakespeare's last will and testament follows. As you will discover, I have played "fast and loose" with the will and its meaning. Those readers seeking a play that sheds light on Shakespeare's writings may be disappointed in my play. So too those audience members who desire a historical representation of Anne Hathaway's life. I have done neither of those things. Instead, I have used the will as a springboard for my own imagination and my artistic goal—to explore the journey of a woman who faces adversity, rises above it, and ultimately re-kindles faith in herself.

—Vern Thiessen
New York City, September, 2007

THE LAST WILL AND TESTEMENT OF SHAKESPEARE

NOTE: The following text of Shakespeare's will has modernized spelling, and a translation of the Latin passages. Words that are struck out in the original will are presented here in ~~strikeout~~ and additions to the will are here represented in CAPS. Sections here in ***bold italics*** indicate parts of the will directly quoted in the play.

—V.T.

Vicesimo Quinto die ~~Januarij~~ Marti Anno Regni Domini nostri Jacobi nunc Regis Anglie &c decimo quarto & Scotie xlix Annoque domini 1616. (*Translation: On the 25th day in the year of the reign of our lord James, King of England, etc., the 14th, and of Scotland the 49th, in the year of our Lord, 1616.*)

T(estamentum) of William Shackspeare.

In the name of God, Amen. I, William Shackspeare of Stratford-upon-Avon in the county of Warwick, gent., in perfect health and memory, God be praised, do make and ordain this my last will and testament in manner and form following. That is to say, first, I commend my soul into the hands of God my Creator, hoping and assuredly believing, through the only merits of Jesus Christ my Saviour, to be made partaker of life everlasting, and my body to the earth whereof it is made.

Item, I give and bequeath unto my ~~Sonne in L~~ ***daughter Judith one hundred and fifty pounds of lawful English money,*** to be paid unto her in the manner and form following; That is to say, one hundred pounds *IN DISCHARGE OF HER MAR-RIAGE PORTION* within one year after my decease, with consideration after the rate of two shillings in the pound for so long time as the same shall be unpaid unto her after my decease, and the fifty pounds residue thereof upon her surrendering OF, or giving of such sufficient security as the overseers of this my will shall like of to surrender or grant, all her estate and right that shall descend or come unto her after my decease, OR THAT SHE now hath of, in, or to one copyhold tenement, with the appurtenances, lying and being in Stratford-upon-Avon aforesaid in the said county of Warwick, being parcel or holden of the manor of Rowington, unto my daughter Susanna Hall and her heirs for ever.

Item, I give and bequeath unto my said daughter Judith one hundred and fifty pounds more, if she or any issue of her body by living at the end of three years next ensuing the day of the date of this my will, during which time my executors are to pay her consideration from my decease according to the rate aforesaid; and if she die within the said term without issue of her body, then my will is, and I do give and bequeath one hundred pounds thereof to my niece, Elizabeth Hall, and the fifty pounds to be set forth by my executors during the life of my sister, Joan Hart, and the use and profit thereof coming shall be paid to my said sister Joan, and after her decease the said fifty pounds shall remain amongst the children of my said sister, equally to be divided amongst them. But if my said daughter Judith be living at the end of the said three years, or any issue of her body, then my will is, and so I devise and bequeath the said hundred and fifty pounds to be set out BY MY EXECUTORS AND OVERSEERS for the best benefit of her and her issue, and THE STOCK not TO BE paid unto her so long as she shall be married and covert baron ~~by my executors and overseers~~; but my will is that she shall have the consideration yearly paid unto her during her life, and, after her decease the said stock and consideration to be paid to her children, if she have any, and not to her executors or assigns, she living the said term after my decease. Provided that if such husband as she shall at the end of the said three years be married unto or attain after do sufficiently assure unto her and the issue of her body lands answerable to the portion by this my will given unto her and to be adjudged so by my executors and overseers, then my will is that the said 150 pounds shall be paid to such husband as shall make such assurance, to his own use.

Item, I give and bequeath unto my said sister Joan 20 pounds and all my wearing apparel, to be paid and delivered within one year after my decease; *and I do will and devise unto her THE HOUSE* with the appurtenances *in Stratford, wherein she dwelleth, for her natural life,* under the yearly rent of twelvepence.

Item, I give and bequeath unto her three sonns, William Hart, —— Hart, and Michael Hart, five pounds a piece, to be paid within one year after my decease ~~to be set out for her within one year after my desceasee by my executors with the advise and directions of my overseers for her best profit until her marriage and then the same with the increase thereof to be paid unto her.~~

Item, I give and bequeath unto THE SAID ELIZABETH HALL, all my plate, EXCEPT MY BROAD SILVER AND GILT BOWL, that I now have at the date of this my will.

Item, I give and bequeath unto the poor of Stratford aforesaid ten pounds; to Mr. Thomas Combe my sword; to Thomas Russell, Esquire, five pounds; and to Francis Collins, of the borough of Warwick in the county of Warwick, gent., thirteen pounds, six shillings, and eightpence, to be paid within one year after my decease.

Item, I give and bequeath *to* ~~Mr. Richard Tyler~~ the elder *HAMLET SADLER 26 s. 8 d. to buy him a ring;* TO WILLIAM REYNOLDS, GENT., 26 S. 8 D. TO BUY HIM A RING; to my godson, William Walker, 20 s. in gold; to Anthony Nashe, gent., 26 s. 8 d. and to Mr John Nashe 26 s. 8 d., *AND TO*

MY FELLOWS JOHN HEMINGS, RICHARD BURBAGE, AND HENRY CONDELL, 26 S. 8 D. A PIECE TO BUY THEM RINGS.

Item, I give, will, bequeath, and devise, unto my daughter Susanna Hall, FOR BETTER ENABLING OF HER TO PERFORM THIS MY WILL AND TOWARDS THE PERFORMANCE THEREOF, all that capital messuage or tenement with the appurtenances, IN STRATFORD AFORE-SAID, called the New Place, wherein I now dwell, and two messuages or tenements with the appurtenances situate, lying, and being in Henley Street, within the borough of Stratford aforesaid; and all my barns, stables, orchards, gardens, lands, tenements, and hereditaments, whatsoever, situate, lying, and being, or to be had, received, perceived, or taken, within the towns, hamlets, villages, fields, and grounds, of Stratford-upon-Avon, Old Stratford, Bushopton, and Welcombe, or in any of them in the said county of Warwick; and also all that messuage or tenement with the appurtenances, wherein one John Robinson dwelleth, situate, lying and being in the Blackfriars in London, near the Wardrobe; and all my other lands, tenements, and hereditaments whatsoever, *to have and to hold* all and singular the said premises, with their appurtenances, unto the said Susanna Hall, for and *during the term of her natural life, and after her decease, to the first son of her body lawfully issuing*, and *to the heirs males of the body* of the said first son lawfully issuing; and for default of such issue to the second son of her body, lawfully issuing, and so to the heirs males of the body of the said second son lawfully issuing; and for default of such heirs, to the third son of the body of the said Susanna lawfully issuing, and of the heirs males of the body of the said third son lawfully issuing; and for default of such issue, the same so to be and remain to the fourth, fifth, sixth, and seventh sons of her body lawfully issuing, one after another, and to the heirs males of the bodies of the bodies of the said fourth, fifth, sixth, and seventh sons lawfully issuing in such manner as it is before limited, to be and remain to the first, second, and third sons of her body, and to their heirs males. And for default of such issue, the said premises to be and remain to my said niece Hall and the heirs males of her body lawfully issuing; and for default of such issue, to my daughter Judith, and the heirs males of her body lawfully issuing; and for default of such issue, to the right heirs of me the said William Shackspeare for ever.

ITEM, I GIVE UNTO MY WIFE MY SECOND BEST BED WITH THE FURNITURE.

Item, I give and bequeath to my said daughter Judith my broad silver gilt bowl. All the rest of *my goods, chattel, leases, plate, jewels, and household stuff whatsoever*, after my debts and legacies paid and my funeral expenses discharged, I give, devise, and bequeath to my son-in-law, John Hall, gent., and my daughter Susanna, his wife, whom I ordain and make executors of this my last will and testament. And I do entreat and appoint THE SAID Thomas Russell, Esquire, and Francis Collins, gent., to be overseers hereof, and do revoke all former wills, and publish this to be my last will and testament. In witness whereof I have hereunto put my ~~seal~~ hand, the day and year first above written by me, William Shakspeare.

Witnesses to the publishing hereof:
Fra: Collins
Julyus Shawe
John Robinson
Hamnet Sadler
Robert Whattcott

Vern Thiessen is one of Canada's most-produced playwrights. His plays have been seen across Canada, the United States, Asia, the United Kingdom, the Middle East and Europe. Well-known works include *Vimy*, *Shakespeare's Will* and *Apple*. *Einstein's Gift*, *A More Perfect Union* and *Lenin's Embalmers* have all been seen off-Broadway. His plays for young audiences include *Bird Brain*, *Dawn Quixote* and *Windmill*. With composer/collaborator Olaf Pyttlik he has created two musicals, *Rich* and *Rapa Nui*. Thiessen is also the author of several adaptations, including *Wuthering Heights*. He is the winner of many awards including the Governor General's Literary Award, Canada's highest honour for playwriting. Thiessen is a past president of the Playwrights Guild of Canada and of the Writers Guild of Alberta. He splits his time between Canada and New York City.